CONTENTS

WELCOME TO THE RAISE YOUR GAME BOOK CLUB.

I hope you enjoy *reading* this book as much as I enjoyed *writing* it. More importantly, I hope you find it to be useful, meaningful, and applicable.

I feel so fortunate to have worked with, learned from, and observed many legendary leaders, consummate teammates, and world-class performers.

I wrote this book to share the concepts, lessons, and strategies I've accumulated over the course of my career, and to translate them in a practical way so you can apply them to your team (and your life).

The purpose of this Book Club is to take a deeper dive into the book's teachings and to spark action that results in improved habits, mindset, and performance.

This program will unpack the book's most pivotal lessons and convert them into tangible action steps to help everyone on your team narrow the gap between *knowing* and *doing*.

Additionally, this resource will allow you to generate productive dialogue that fosters a stronger connection with the members of your team. Connection creates caring—and caring matters.

This Book Club is only intended to be a framework. Ultimately, it will be your efforts, direction and commitment as a facilitator to empower the members of your team to raise *their* game. The result will be individual and organizational upward shifts in awareness, communication, and culture.

Keep in mind—a lot of people *buy* books. An alarmingly low percentage actually *read* them. An even smaller percentage use what they read and put it into action! I don't want that to be you or those on your team.

As I said in the book, knowledge by itself is not powerful. True power only comes from the *application* of that knowledge. Knowledge unapplied is useless.

Reading this book without executing its lessons will have the same effect as not reading it at all. The only way you will *Raise Your Game* is to take the concepts from this book and put them into practice.

This Book Club will assist you in doing just that. Teams that *read* together, *win* together.

It's time to Raise Your Game!

About This Facilitator Guide

You have full control over how you run your Book Club, the guidelines below are simply suggestions. Book Clubs can become a part of your weekly team meetings or you can run them at separate times. You know your team best. Do what is sustainable and what will achieve the best results for your team.

With that being said, each chapter has discussions and short exercises you can execute. They are broken into 3 sections that allow you to customize your Book Club depending on the amount of time you have available. There are 5 Minute Quick Takes, 15 Minute Exercises, and Group Discussion Questions that could take 20+ minutes depending on how deep you take them or how many questions you choose to dive into.

LOGISTICS

We recommend that you make a commitment to meet in-person, once a week. Assigning one chapter per week will keep the material fresh and moving at a steady pace, and generate positive momentum.

STANDARDS

The impact and overall experience of this Book Club will be in direct proportion to the standards (guidelines) you set and how well the group upholds them. We recommend that you conduct an initial meeting so the group can have input in forming these standards. People will always have more focus, give more effort, and have more buy-in to things they help create!

Here are a few sample standards:

1. We agree to read the chapter and complete the assignment prior to each session

2. We will bring our book (and workbook)

3. We will share openly, honestly, and respectfully

4. We will eliminate distractions (put away phones) and stay fully present

LAUNCH

Hold an initial meeting to accomplish the following:

- Explain why you are doing this and how they will benefit
- Introduce the facilitators/groups, format, and timeline
- Establish standards and allow for questions/concerns
- Distribute books and workbooks

PART ONE

PLAYER

A player is any individual who is part of a team, company, or organization. Everyone participating is considered a player.

Chapter 1: Self-Awareness

CHAPTER HIGHLIGHTS

- Make "you" your business
- Self-awareness means having and developing an understanding of who you are and what you can and can't do
- There are 2 things you have 100% control over: your attitude and your effort
- Identify what you do best and double down on it

FACILITATOR NOTE

Self-awareness is a topic that requires vulnerability to discuss. While it's critical to have it as a first chapter, it also provides a challenge as the first session. You set the stage for the discussion. Start it off by sharing what you discovered about yourself as you completed the self-tests. Share your strength, your weakness, and the one thing you're doing to continuously work on yourself. Ask the team to help hold you accountable. Do this before you jump into the session and your team will feel more at ease.

QUICK TAKES (5 MINUTES)

Pick one question to pose to the group.

1. Think back to the story of John Wooden teaching his players how to put on their socks and shoes. It was about managing the basics. On our team, what are the basics, or the equivalent to putting on your socks and shoes correctly to avoid blisters?

2. Simon Sinek believes we've lost the ability to excel in one thing. What's one thing you believe you do that no one else can on this team? Or what's one thing this team does that is invaluable? If you can't identify one thing, what's one thing we could we do to make ourselves invaluable? Explain.

EXERCISE (15 MINUTES)

Instructions: Ask 1 person (target) to stand. Go around the group and ask each person to directly tell the "target" what they believe their strength to be.

This is an exercise in team vulnerability as well as an exercise to create awareness around specific strengths.

After each person has had a chance to play "target," ask each individual if the strength(s) identified was/were what they believed their top strength(s) to be.

GROUP DISCUSSION (20+ MINUTES)

Use these series of questions to lead a discussion:

1. What's one anecdote that stood out to you as you read this chapter? Explain.

2. What do you believe the most detrimental weakness would be for a player? Explain.

3. Being self-aware 100% of the time is extremely difficult. What do you find most challenging to implement from this chapter?

4. What strengths do people have on this team that aren't being utilized? Is there a way to incorporate them?

5. Here's a hypothetical scenario: A teammate's "blind spot" is negatively affecting the team. How do you approach this?

FACILITATOR NOTE

You can build out the scenario in Question 5 to apply specifically to your team. Don't be afraid to challenge answers and continue the discussion

DO THE WORK

- The self-tests from this chapter were extensive. Ask your team if they completed them all. If not, ask them what's holding them back? Self-awareness is essential for team success. If they haven't completed the self-tests, encourage individuals to complete them.

- Read the next chapter (Passion) and complete that portion of the workbook before the next session.

Chapter 2: Passion

CHAPTER HIGHLIGHTS

- Passion is the engine that powers us through what we have to do
- If you don't know what your passion is, commit to finding it
- Passion is what will separate you from others
- Skill alone rarely gets the job done
- Your attitude and approach determine whether it's a "grind" or a journey
- Care about the result so much that you are willing to do what it takes to get there
- Use your passion as a guide to what you should be doing

QUICK TAKES (5 MINUTES)

Alan defines hard work as intentionally leaving your comfort zone with purpose. You need hard work to be successful. Where are we staying in our comfort zone as a team (or as individuals)? How is staying in this comfort zone limiting our growth? What could happen if we reach beyond our comfort zone and what does that look like for our team?

EXERCISE (15 MINUTES)

Instructions: Ask your team to call out the skills and/or knowledge that are invaluable to the team. Write all the things down on a whiteboard or flipchart.

Now, everyone has a list of things that "need to be done" on the team. Ask everyone to identify one item on the board they're passionate about (even if they don't currently do it today).

Challenge them to become the master of the knowledge/skill they identified.

DISCUSSION

1. Who do you know who is passionate? What makes you believe they are passionate? What things do they do or not do?

2. What did you think about framing things from "have to" to "get to"?

3. What motivates you beyond winning or money? What motivates this team?

4. What are some obstacles that we're facing as a team or that you're facing as an individual on this team? How do we turn those obstacles into fuel?

DO THE WORK

Read the next chapter (Discipline) and complete that portion of the workbook before the next session.

Chapter 3: Discipline

CHAPTER HIGHLIGHTS

- Discipline means having and maintaining a system in place to refine and work on your game
- You create your own success by building habits to reach it
- Consistent habits make the best the best—build your own structure of habit
- Spend your time wisely and efficiently; trim the "fat" from your day
- Make the most of your time and focus on what matters

QUICK TAKES (5 MINUTES)

What are the three most important things we do as a team? Are these the things we actually do every day?

If yes, great.

If no, let's consider what we can do to become more efficient and productive.

EXERCISE (15 MINUTES)

Instructions: Pose the following questions and write down the responses of your team next to each item on a whiteboard or flipchart.

Alan says there are 6 things you can do to be prepared:

1. Read
2. Study
3. Observe
4. Evaluate
5. Reach Out
6. Risk

Specifically, what does that mean in our world, on our team? What/who should we be reading, studying, observing, reaching out to, risking?

Email your team their responses and challenge them to have the discipline to prepare in these 6 areas. There are no excuses now that they know the what and the who.

GROUP DISCUSSION

1. What do you believe we can improve to become a more efficient and productive team?

2. What's an area in your life where you struggle with discipline (working out, reading, diet, etc.)? Why do you think that area is a struggle?

3. Think back to Steph Curry needing to swish the ball, not just make the shot. What's a swish for you? What's a swish for this team?

4. Kobe Bryant practices the most basic drills and he's one of the best. What could we practice more? What basic drills should we be running?

5. Alan's friend Dave went to scout players, but he wasn't looking at how they played in the game. Instead, he was looking at how they interacted with their coach and teammates, how they talked to the staff, and what routines they executed. If someone observed us as a team, what would they find? Are there moments we wouldn't be proud of in our past?

6. Alan says, "Not working hard is a choice." What do you think about this after reading the chapter?

DO THE WORK

Read the next chapter (Coachability) and complete that portion of the workbook before the next session.

Chapter 4: Coachability

CHAPTER HIGHLIGHTS

- The successful ones never stop growing
- Accept that you have more to learn and be willing to get it from anywhere and anyone
- You control your "knowledge advantage"
- Never judge who is worth paying attention to
- Train your eyes to recognize the good ideas all around you
- Embrace failure as a teaching tool
- Feedback is the sound of the world responding to you

QUICK TAKES (5 MINUTES)

"If you aren't dropping the ball, you aren't getting any better." What does this quote mean to our team? How do we know our limits and push past them?

EXERCISE (15 MINUTES)

Instructions: Ask your team to call out all the negative feedback they've received—things that they may have been defensive about or shrugged off—even if they sound ridiculous. Write them all down on a whiteboard or flipchart.

After you've compiled a list, ask them:

- How did these make you feel in the moment?
- How did you react in the moment?
- How do you feel now looking back on those times?
- Is there truth here? Are there patterns emerging?
- What can we learn from this feedback, even if it doesn't feel good?

GROUP DISCUSSION (20+ MINUTES)

1. Can you share a time when you received feedback, implemented it, and things improved?

2. Coachability breaks down to three parts: Trust, Openness, and Execution. Which one do you perceive is the most difficult? Why?

3. Kevin Durant said, "Off-season is the real season." What could we be doing during that time that we aren't now?

4. What's one thing you're curious about that we aren't doing today?

5. Failure is valuable. Can you share a story about a time when you failed and what you learned? Has the team ever failed? What did we learn? How can we fail better next time?

6. Who on the team has exhibited coachability? How?

7. How can we put into practice Frank Shamrock's +, =, - system on our team?

DO THE WORK

Read the next chapter (Confidence) and complete that portion of the workbook before the next session.

Chapter 5: Confidence

CHAPTER HIGHLIGHTS

- Self-Awareness + Passion + Discipline + Coachability = Confidence
- Earned confidence is a result of knowing yourself, caring about what you do, and committing to getting better
- There's nothing more damaging than false confidence and nothing more powerful than properly grounded confidence
- Confidence is a contagious force that shines a light on your work and gives energy to others
- Don't be a jerk, but make sure your confidence comes through in how you talk and do your work
- Earned confidence is a magnetic force that will get you what you want

QUICK TAKES (5 MINUTES)

Alan says there's a difference between confidence and arrogance. Where's that line? How do you know you haven't crossed it?

EXERCISE (15 MINUTES)

Instructions: Present the scenario with your team and ask them how they would handle the situation. You can also ask them to roleplay the conversation in groups of 2.

Scenario: A teammate's confidence has crossed over into arrogance, and it's hurting the team. Morale is down and people aren't working well together. How do you resolve this situation?

At the end of the exercise, ask your team how it felt from both sides. Would they be willing to tackle this head-on if it was really happening on the team?

GROUP DISCUSSION (20+ MINUTES)

1. If confidence comes from experience and knowledge, in what areas should this team have confidence?

2. Confidence is built by both winning and losing. If you had to compare the two in your own life, which do you believe gives you more confidence in the long-run?

3. What routines have you developed that build your confidence?

4. Out of the seven things Alan learned on Stratton Mountain, which resonates with you the most and why?

5. What's been the biggest lesson you've taken from the first section of the book?

DO THE WORK

Read the next chapter (Vision) and complete that portion of the workbook before the next session.

PART TWO

COACH

In the book, a "coach" refers to someone who has been given authority over others. For the purposes of this Book Club, each individual should consider the way they lead themselves, and also how the chapters apply to the team.

Chapter 6: Vision

CHAPTER HIGHLIGHTS

- In order to move forward, you must envision what you want to create, then you can take the steps to make it happen

- Vision is understanding your purpose and funneling everything you do towards that ultimate goal

- Take into account big-picture thinking—how today is connected to yesterday and tomorrow

- Don't chase a popular idea, create the right idea

QUICK TAKES (5 MINUTES)

Alan talks about court vision, meaning players always position themselves to see as much of the court as possible. They also have to think one or two plays ahead to anticipate where defenders will shift or where teammates will cut to. How can we translate these same strategies on our team?

EXERCISE (15 MINUTES)

Instructions: Instructions: Ask the team to identify the difference(s) between function vs. purpose and write their responses on a whiteboard or flipchart. When you've come up with a purpose the team can agree on, email it to the group after the meeting.

Dr. Brian Williams said, "A chair's function is to provide a place for someone to sit. A chair's purpose is to provide comfort." Let's not confuse our function for our purpose.

What is our team's function? What is our purpose?

GROUP DISCUSSION (20+ MINUTES)

1. Do you know what our team vision is? How about our purpose [If you didn't do the Exercise above]?

   a. If not, let's talk about where we are headed. Where do you think we are headed? Where should we be headed? What's our purpose? Then, what's our vision for the future?

2. Vision isn't just about the team vision, it's also about setting your own vision for your future. Does anyone have a personal vision statement they'd like to share?

3. Vision is seeing things before they happen or before people could even consider they could happen. But hindsight is 20/20. How do you know your vision is the right vision? What are some signs to look for?

4. Alan says, "Your comfort zone is your cage." Protecting a lead doesn't work. What's the lead we are protecting? Is there something we are holding onto that's holding us back from achieving more?

5. If you had to sum up in one word what this team does, what would it be? Think back to Apple. Their word was simplicity.

DO THE WORK

Read the next chapter (Culture) and complete that portion of the workbook before the next session.

Chapter 7: Culture

CHAPTER HIGHLIGHTS

- Culture is the collective values, beliefs, behaviors, and environment of a team, group, or organization

- Culture is the environment (both physical and psychological) that a leader creates to keep his or her people motivated, committed, and secure

- Culture is spread and maintained by everyone

- It's a leader's job to prepare the soil that will maximize others' potential and encourage them to be as productive as possible

- A leader who creates a strong culture knows it's not about forcing people to follow you—it's about making them want to

- All leaders must create a culture of respect for everyone to thrive

- A group's culture is best reflected through how members act when the leader is not around

QUICK TAKES (5 MINUTES)

Building meaningful relationships is the most effective way to keep your team grounded, connected, and motivated. If relationships are the foundation for a winning culture, how can we form better relationships? What creates good relationships among team members?

EXERCISE (15 MINUTES)

Instructions: Use a whiteboard or flipchart. Present this scenario:

Imagine someone is trying out for our team and they ask, "What's the culture like?" What's your DREAM response?

Write down their answers. After you've compiled them all, ask if they believe the list applies to the team TODAY? If not, can they all commit to this type of culture? What needs to happen to make this a reality?

GROUP DISCUSSION (20+ MINUTES)

1. What does an excellent culture look like to you? Who has the best culture out of any **team** you know and why?

2. What are the major strengths on this team?

3. If you heard someone (a **person** on another team) describe our team culture as it stands today, what would they say? Would you be proud to hear their response?

4. What's lacking in our current culture that needs to be present?

5. If someone is being negative, what's the best way to squash the behavior? We are all responsible for culture on this team, so what would you do?

DO THE WORK

Read the next chapter (Servant) and complete that portion of the workbook before the next session.

Chapter 8: Servant

CHAPTER HIGHLIGHTS

- A leader serves his or her people, not the other way around
- It's impossible to be both selfish and an effective leader
- A leader is committed to adding value to everyone they come in contact with
- Don't treat others the way you want to be treated. Treat them the way they want to be treated

QUICK TAKES (5 MINUTES)

After reading about all the servant leaders and their examples, have you experienced one in your lifetime? What did they do that made them a servant leader?

EXERCISE (15 MINUTES)

Instructions: Use a whiteboard or flipchart. On one side write "more of," on the other side write "less of." Ask your team to answer these questions and list their answers under the respective columns.

What do you do that you want to do more of?

What do you do that you want to do less of?

After you've made the list, ask them what they think you can do with this new knowledge. What can you do collectively to make the list a reality?

GROUP DISCUSSION (20+ MINUTES)

1. What does a servant leader look like to you? What would they do specifically to help you?

2. Why do you believe many people find serving others difficult? What are the challenges?

3. Which leader story in this chapter stood out to you and why?

4. Alan talked about treating people as equals vs. treating them the same. What do you feel this means? How can we treat each other equally, yet not the same?

5. While not everyone leads a team, that doesn't stop you from being a servant to your team or others. What ideas do you have for how to live this out in our team?

DO THE WORK

Read the next chapter (Character) and complete that portion of the workbook before the next session.

Chapter 9: Character

QUICK TAKES (5 MINUTES)

Who do you know that exhibits great character? Explain what they do.

EXERCISE (15 MINUTES)

Instructions: Our character is constantly being tested. Have your team come up with some character-testing situations. Then discuss the easy way to handle them vs. the way to handle them with character.

GROUP DISCUSSION (20+ MINUTES)

1. If someone like Coach K can take the time to write handwritten notes, what can we do as a team to go the extra mile and share our character?

2. Character isn't about waiting around for a reward; it's about doing what you believe is right. What types of things do you do that are just a part of who you are?

3. What's something you're inspired to start doing after reading this chapter?

4. Can you think of a time when someone showed their true character and how it impacted you positively or negatively?

5. When was a time your character was tested? Maybe no one was watching and you had to make a decision about what to do?

DO THE WORK

Read the next chapter (Empowerment) and complete that portion of the workbook before the next session.

Chapter 10: Empowerment

CHAPTER HIGHLIGHTS

- Successful leaders trust the "car they built," and they are comfortable delegating and letting others lead

- A measurement of a true leader is to see if he/she is producing other high-quality leaders

- Empowering others creates "buy-in"—a vested interest in the mission

- It takes tremendous security, trust, and confidence for a leader to hand the reins off, but it's vital

- Empowerment is the opposite of micromanaging

QUICK TAKES (5 MINUTES)

Do we truly encourage empowerment and appropriate autonomy? What are some real challenges stopping us?

EXERCISE (15 MINUTES)

Instructions: Empowerment is closely tied to self-awareness: being able to know what you can and cannot do well, and also knowing the best use of your time. For this exercise, break everyone into groups of 2 or 3 and have them discuss:

- One thing they don't do it well

- One thing they do that isn't the best use of their time

- One thing they are the best at it

Check the answers with your partner(s) to make sure they agree (because they also know you really well).

GROUP DISCUSSION (20+ MINUTES)

1. Tell us about a time when you felt empowered. What was the result?

2. Where are you feeling the most frustrated as a team? What can we do to fix it?

3. If you're scared to let someone else do something, why do you think that is? What's your underlying concern? Is it REAL?

4. What's a habit we can begin implementing to help us become a more empowered team? Or a team of empowerers?

DO THE WORK

Read the next chapter (Belief) and complete that portion of the workbook before the next session.

PART THREE

TEAM

A team is any group, organization, or company that works together to achieve a common goal.

Chapter 11: Belief

CHAPTER HIGHLIGHTS

- A team comes together over a collective belief in an idea and a mission
- Success comes when commitment meets belief
- Set goals that are both realistic and just out of reach—belief will help you cross the divide
- The best leaders are able to cultivate a powerful feeling of belief within the team and tap into it consistently
- Lack of belief from one player can pull everyone and everything down
- Create a sense of accountability: if a rule doesn't exist for one, it doesn't exist at all

QUICK TAKES (5 MINUTES)

Think about how you feel when you wake up in the morning. Out of the time you've spent on this team, which day were you excited about the most? What were you doing that day? Why were you excited?

EXERCISE (15 MINUTES)

Instructions: Present the following scenario in stages to initiate a conversation:

Part 1: We have standards on this team. What is the most critical standard we have on this team?

Part 2: Imagine someone isn't meeting the standard we just identified. How do we hold them accountable?

GROUP DISCUSSION (20+ MINUTES)

1. Tom Izzo had his players cut the net down at the beginning of the season to get them thinking about something bigger. What would be our equivalent of cutting down the net?

2. What are some realistic, yet currently out of reach goals we have as a team?

3. If someone is expressing a lack of belief, how should we address it?

4. What are the standards we have on our team?

5. How can we create a culture of accountability on our team so we can all feel comfortable holding each other to the high standards we have?

DO THE WORK

Read the next chapter (Unselfishness) and complete that portion of the workbook before the next session.

Chapter 12: Unselfishness

CHAPTER HIGHLIGHTS

- A team is made or broken based on how much each member is willing to sacrifice self-interest and self-glory for team success

- A team is a group of people who put the group's needs ahead of his or her own

- Each of us has an instinctive drive towards self-interest. A team puts this aside in service of a larger goal

- A group finds success when they eliminate "you versus me" and replace it with "you plus me." With that mindset 1+1 = 3

- Unselfishness has been proven as an effective approach to achieving and succeeding

QUICK TAKES (5 MINUTES)

When have people on this team exhibited unselfishness? Give specific examples.

EXERCISE (15 MINUTES)

Instructions: Break into groups of 2-4 people. Have participants share one of three things with each person in their small group:

- Someone you know who may benefit them (ask if they'd like an introduction)
- Something you know that may add value to them (a book recommendation, article, video, an app, or even a process)
- What you can do to help them (after you inquire how they're doing)

This is a practice in giving.

GROUP DISCUSSION (20+ MINUTES)

1. What does unselfishness mean to you?

2. There's a myth that givers get trampled, but it's just that, a myth. Can you think of times when givers won your respect?

3. Who are some givers you've known in your life? What did they do for you?

4. How do you balance ambition with unselfishness?

5. What does 1+1 = 3 look like on our team?

DO THE WORK

Read the next chapter (Role Clarity) and complete that portion of the workbook before the next session.

Chapter 13: Role Clarity

CHAPTER HIGHLIGHTS

- A team is an interlocking puzzle where each shape and size is distinct, necessary, and valuable to the whole

- Role clarity comes from the leader; accepting and embracing that role is up to the individual

- Begin with fulfilling your current role

- Spend extra time earning an expanded or new role

- It's vital to acknowledge the so-called role players

- Don't assume a collection of top talent will automatically generate success. Becoming a unit involves an understanding and acceptance of roles

QUICK TAKES (5 MINUTES)

Tell me about a time when you were on this team (or another team) and during a pivotal moment, everyone knew their role and the team won because of it.

EXERCISE (15 MINUTES)

Instructions: Use a whiteboard or flipchart. On one side write "name" on the other side write "strength." List each person under "name" and ask the team to identify one unique, role-based strength for each person in the room. The challenge is not to have overlap.

Afterwards, pose a challenge to the group: find ways to best utilize each person's skill for the team's benefit.

GROUP DISCUSSION (20+ MINUTES)

1. What challenges arise when people don't have a clear role?

2. Jeremy Lin seemed to have more fun playing a role on a team than being the star player. What does it feel like for you when the team gets in lockstep?

3. If someone is performing the role they want, and not their current role, what can we do as a group to help them?

4. How can we collectively acknowledge all the players on the team for their roles, versus just acknowledging those who might be "star players"?

5. How do you embrace your role?

DO THE WORK

Read the next chapter (Communication) and complete that portion of the workbook before the next session.

Chapter 14: Communication

CHAPTER HIGHLIGHTS

- A team doesn't know what it doesn't share with each other

- Communication ensures teams will catch dissent, role conflict, or disunity before it becomes unmanageable

- Our ideas and emotions are constantly in flux. The best communication is open, honest, and consistent

- Communication is about trust

- The most important and often forgotten form of communication is listening

- Think about the most appropriate form of communication for a person or situation rather than the one that's most convenient

QUICK TAKES (5 MINUTES)

Alan says that good teams talk and great teams communicate. He's even come up with a rating system to help evaluate and improve communication:

1 - Silent

2 - Noise

3 - Generic Talk

4 - Specific Talk

5 - Directing

On average, what would you rate our team's communication? Explain.

EXERCISE (15 MINUTES)

Instructions: Break into groups of 2-3 people. Have participants role play this scenario using the Six Steps to Mastering Tough Conversations.

Your teammate is slacking off and not mentally showing up every day. Their lack of commitment is starting to impact you.

Step 1: Create a Safe Environment

Step 2: Keep it Professional

Step 3: Be Respectful

Step 4: Watch Your Language

Step 5: Empathize and Clarify

Step 6: End Strong

GROUP DISCUSSION (20+ MINUTES)

1. What communication challenges do we currently have on our team?

2. What's the most challenging part about active listening?

3. Why is it so important to customize your message to the person/situation?

4. We can construct a perfect conversation from a delivery perspective. How do you improve on receiving information that might not be what you expected?

5. Let's practice positive communication. Let's go around the room and say one specific thing you appreciate about each person. Everyone gets a turn and everyone must volunteer at least one positive.

DO THE WORK

Read the next chapter (Cohesion) and complete that portion of the workbook before the next session.

Chapter 15: Cohesion

CHAPTER HIGHLIGHTS

- A cohesive unit operates in sync and as a single unit, through a combination of unselfishness, belief, clear roles, and communication

- The best teams are like a puzzle: different but complementary pieces create the final picture—one missing piece and the puzzle is incomplete

- Great teams suffer and celebrate together

- There are few things in life more satisfying than a team coming together to achieve something they couldn't do individually

QUICK TAKES (5 MINUTES)

Tell me about your favorite time when this team came together to achieve something we couldn't do individually.

EXERCISE (15 MINUTES)

Instructions: Use a whiteboard or flipchart and list out: Communication, Belief, Unselfishness, and Clear Roles. For each of the 4 items listed, what is something an ideal teammate would bring in regards to each one?

GROUP DISCUSSION (20+ MINUTES)

1. Where can this team get better cohesion?

2. How can we increase cohesion as a team?

3. What part of cohesion is the most challenging for you?

4. Taking time to celebrate victories is important. What's a victory you've had this week or this month that you'd like to share and celebrate with the team?

5. What's one area or thing you'd like someone to "assist" you with? Now is the time to ask for help.